Self Portrait

Draw a picture of yourself here.

Art by Jack Desrocher

Balloon Bunch

Trace the lines from the balloons to the kids.
Which balloon is yellow?

Art by Pierre Collet-Derby

Construction Climb

Draw a line from each construction worker to the ground to help them get down. Which ladder is the shortest?

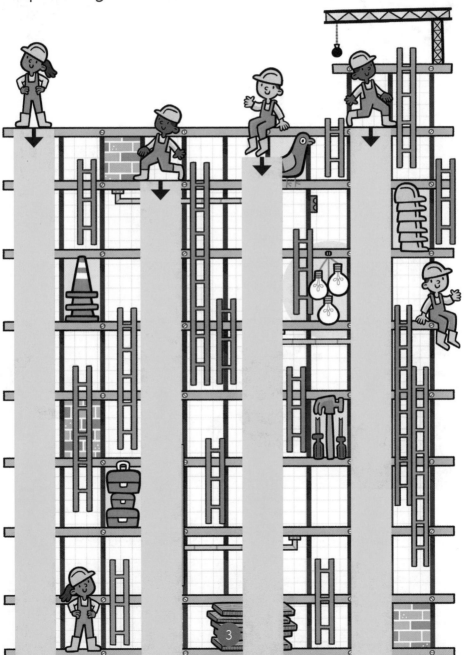

Towering Towers

Trace the lines from the princesses to their friends.
Which tower is the tallest?

Art by Pierre Collet-Derby

Slow Sloths

Draw lines to help the sloths climb the trees.
How many sloths do you see?

Art by Cale Atkinson

Friendly Scarecrow

Trace the lines between the birds and the scarecrow.
What is a scarecrow made out of?

Plant Paths

Draw lines between the plants and the seeds.
What do plants need to grow?

Art by Tom Woolley

Parking Lot

Trace the lines from the cars to their parking spots.
What color are the cars?

Safari Friends

Draw a line from each animal to its baby.
Which animal has stripes?

Birds on a Wire

Trace the lines to give the birds somewhere to perch.
How many birds are on each wire?

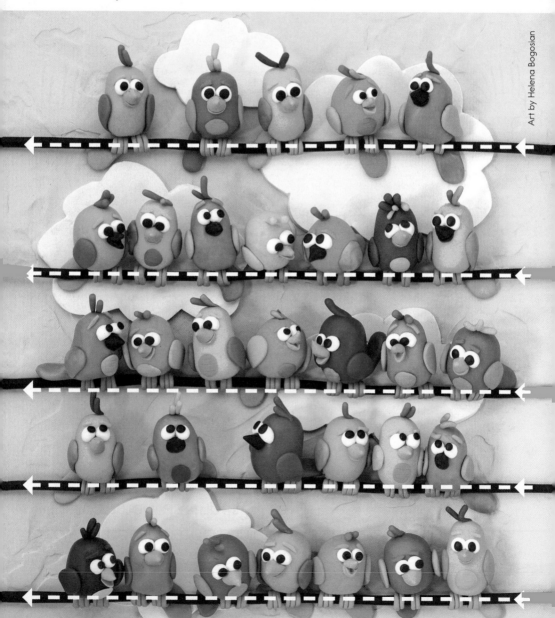

Art by Helena Bogosian

A Day at the Park

Draw lines to show how the squirrels scamper.
What other words begin with **S**?

Art by Jan Bryan-Hunt

On the Road

Trace the lines to show how the trucks travel.
What trucks do you see in your neighborhood?

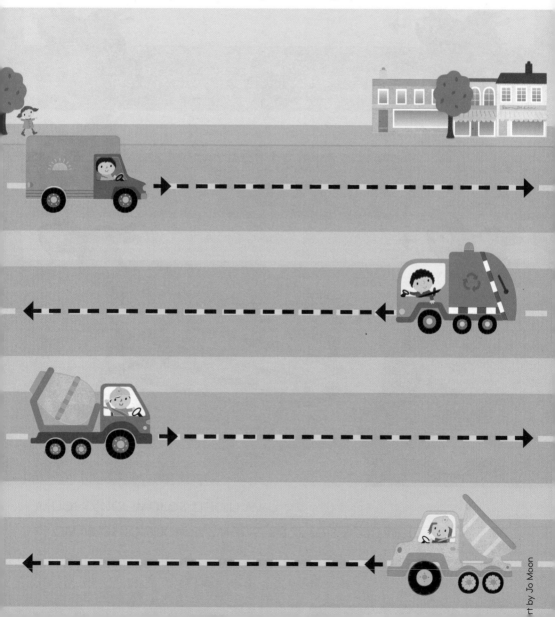

rt by Jo Moon

Playtime

Draw a line from each animal to its toy.
What is your favorite toy?

Art by Barbara Nascimbeni

Tractor Ride

Help the tractor get back to the barn by tracing a path through the maze. What other things might you see on a farm?

START

FINISH

Time to Splash!

Help the lion find his way to the lake by tracing a path through the maze. What other words begin with **L**?

START

FINISH

15

Art by Ivanke and Lola

Birdhouses

Trace the lines from the birds to the birdhouses.
Which bird is red?

Up the Hill

Draw lines to help the llamas get to their mamas.
What do you call your mama?

Art by Anna Jones

Kayaking Yaks

Trace the lines from the yaks to the river.
What are some things that float?

Art by Josh Cleland

Downhill Skiers

Draw lines to help the bunnies ski down the hill.
What winter activities do you like to do?

Art by Mike Brownlow

Critter Matching

Draw a line from each critter to its match.
Where do you think these animals live?

Sea Horse Matching

Draw a line from each sea horse to its match.
How many pairs did you find?

Soccer Stars

Trace the lines to show how the soccer ball moves.
What sports do you like?

Crab Walk

Draw lines to show how the crabs walk across the sand. What else might you see at the beach?

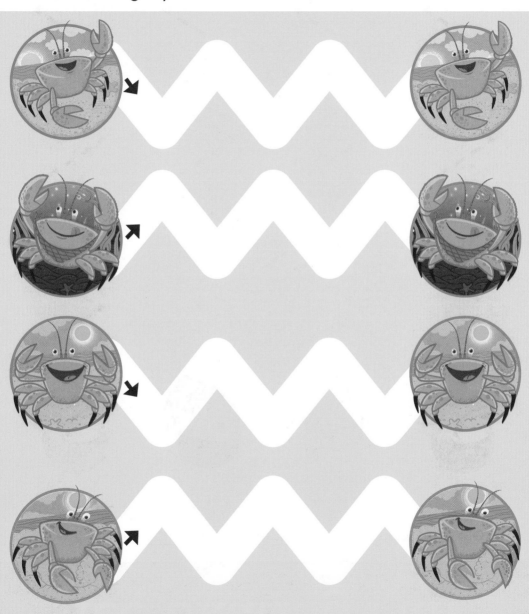

Art by Mitch Mortimer

Ice-Skating Fun

Trace the lines to help the ice skaters get across the ice.
Why do ice skaters wear skates?

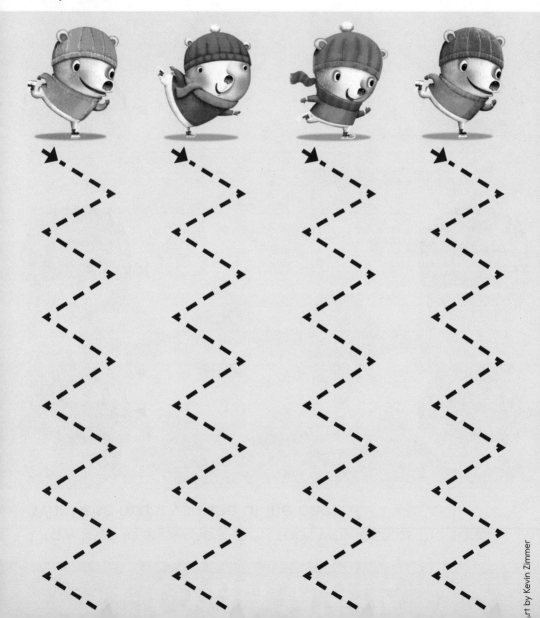

Flight Paths

Draw a line to show how the hot-air balloons will get down to the ground. What other things fly?

Art by Mike Moran

Bakery Treats

Draw an ✖ to cross out the dessert in each row that doesn't match the others. What is your favorite treat?

Art by Anette Heiberg

On the Farm

Draw an ✖ to cross out the animal in each row that doesn't match the others. Which animal is pink?

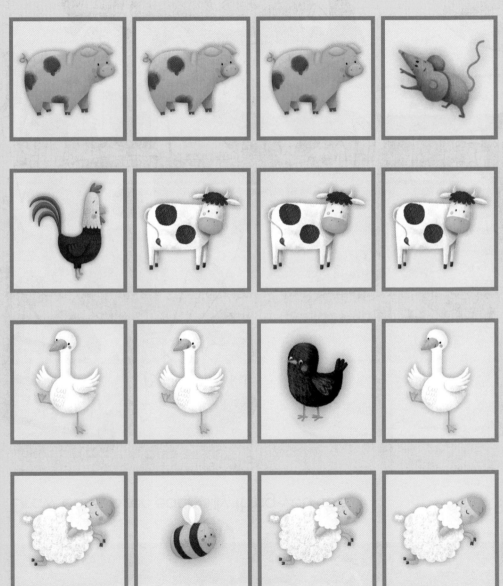

Art by Anna Jones

That's Silly!™

Draw an ✗ over each silly thing you see.

That's Silly!

Draw an ✖ over each silly thing you see.

Art by Katie McDee

Laundry Day

Trace the lines to finish the clothesline.
How many bees can you count?

Umbrellas Up!

Trace the lines over the umbrellas and rainbow.
Which umbrella is blue?

Art by Jackie Stafford

Bunny Hops

Trace the lines to show how the bunnies hop.
What other animals hop?

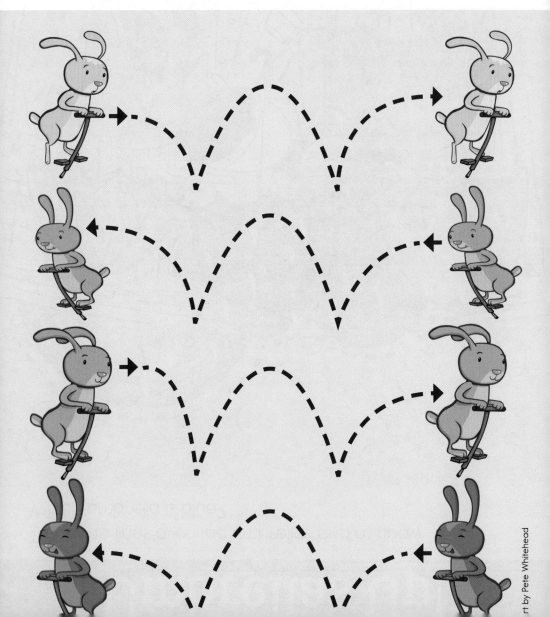

Go Bananas

Draw a line between each pair of monkeys.
Which two monkeys are wearing the same outfit?

33

Fishing Fun

Trace the lines from the fishing poles to the fish.
Which item is not a fish?

Flying Bugs

Trace the lines from the insects to the flowers.

Art by Jo Brown

Look and Look Again

How are these pictures different? Draw a circle around each difference you find. We did three to get you started.

37

Dragonfly

Trace the lines to complete the picture.

Ant Maze

Help the ant get out of the ant hill by tracing a path through the maze. How many ants can you count?

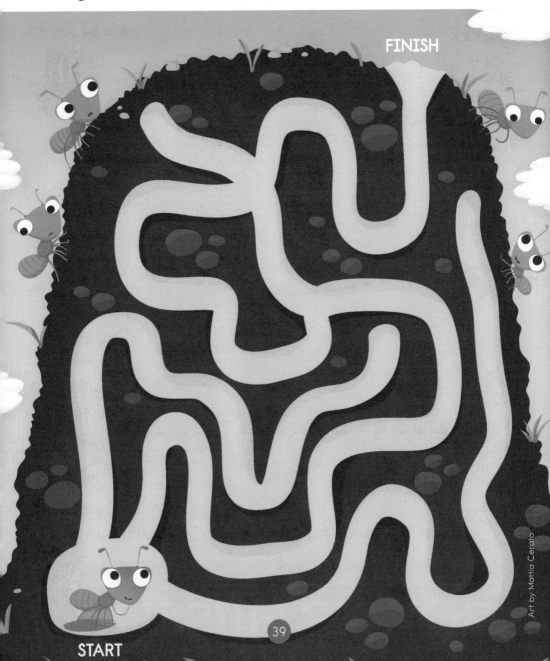

FINISH

START

Art by Mattia Cerato

Tell Silly Stories

Trace or draw your own lines to tell some silly stories.
Then tell your own silly story.

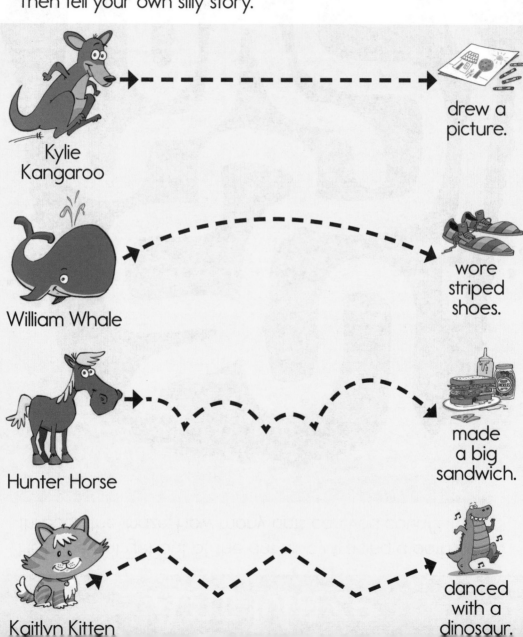

Kylie
Kangaroo

drew a
picture.

William Whale

wore
striped
shoes.

Hunter Horse

made
a big
sandwich.

Kaitlyn Kitten

danced
with a
dinosaur.

Gracie Goat → **wore a puple hat.**

Ava Ant **won first place.**

Gabriel Gorilla **ate a muffin.**

Charles Chipmunk **went shopping.**

Art by Rico Schacherl

Knitting Club

Trace the lines to see what everyone is knitting.
What is something you can make?

Flying Kites

Draw a line from each kid to each kite.
What other things can fly?

Art by Tracy Bishop

Space Race

Help the astronaut find his way to the purple planet.
How many planets do you see?

START

FINISH

Meow Maze

Help the mother cats find their kittens.
What sound do cats make?

Art by Helena Bogosian

Lots of Bots

Trace a line through all the robots from START to FINISH.

START

FINISH

Many Monsters

Trace a line through all the monsters from START to FINISH.

START

FINISH

Art by Dave Clegg

Circles

A circle is round. Trace the circle.
Draw a circle on your own.

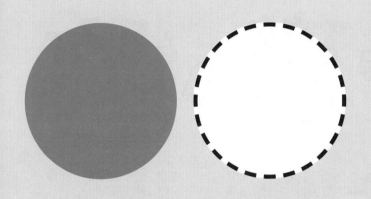

Trace the circles to finish the picture.

Sports Equipment

Trace the circles to finish the picture. Can you find all **11** objects in this Hidden Pictures® puzzle?

Art by Steve Mack

 birdcage

 button

 lollipop

 doughnut

 cookie

 spoon

49

 bowtie

 ruler

 slice of pizza

 egg

ice pop

Squares

A square has four sides that are the same length.
Trace the square. Draw a square on your own.

Trace the squares to finish the picture.

Art Gallery

Trace the squares to finish the picture. Can you find all **12** objects in this Hidden Pictures® puzzle?

orange wheel pear jewel traffic light can butterfly

worm car 51 spoon briefcase pan

Art by Linda Davick

Rectangles

A rectangle has two long sides and two short sides.
Trace the rectangle. Draw a rectangle on your own.

Trace the rectangles to finish the picture.

Art by Jannie Ho

Stamp Collection

Trace the rectangles to finish the picture. Can you find all **11** objects in this Hidden Pictures® puzzle?

Art by Steve Mack

pencil

heart

light bulb

mug

egg

moon

53

bowl

macaroni

ladder

broom

baseball

Triangles

A triangle has three sides. Trace the triangle.
Draw a triangle on your own.

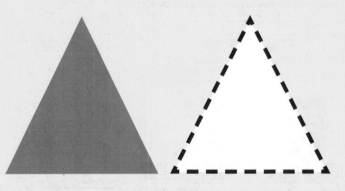

Trace the triangles
to finish the picture.

Happy Birthday!

Trace the triangles to finish the picture. Can you find all **12** objects in this Hidden Pictures® puzzle?

Art by Steve Mack

 ice pop

 olive

pencil

needle

 football

 ladder

 button

 acorn

 lock

slice of bread

 baseball

 wedge of lemon

Monster Apartments

Trace the shapes to finish the drawing. How many squares can you find? How many circles? What other shapes can you find?

Art by Genie Espinosa

Dinosaur Shapes

Trace the shapes to finish the dinosaurs.

Art by Steve Mack

Animal Patterns

Draw stripes and spots on these animals.

Art by Steve Mack

Butterflies

Trace lines to finish the butterfly. Then draw your own.
What else might be in the sky? Draw a picture of it here.

Buildings

Trace the lines to finish the buildings. Then draw your own building. What might you see walking down this sidewalk?

Art by Becka Moor

Say Cheese!

What is this octopus taking a picture of? Draw it here.
Can you find all **7** objects in this Hidden Pictures® puzzle?

pencil

canoe

cherry

lollipop

eyeglasses

ruler

spool of thread

Art by Rob McClurkan

Crazy Car Wash

What silly things do you see at this car wash?
Circle each silly thing, then draw some of your own.

CAR WASH

REX

9.5

Art by Mitch Mortimer

Answers

Page 49 Sports Equipment

Page 51 Art Gallery

Page 53 Stamp Collection

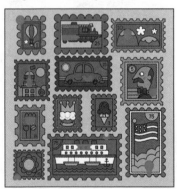

Page 55 Happy Birthday!

Page 62 Say Cheese!